FANGBONE!

THIRD-GRADE BARBARIAN

MICHAEL REX

G. P. PUTNAM'S SONS AN IMPRINT OF PENGUIN GROUP (USA) INC.

G. P. PUTNAM'S SONS

A DIVISION OF PENGUIN YOUNG READERS GROUP.

PUBLISHED BY THE PENGUIN GROUP.

PENGUIN GROUP (USA) INC., 375 HUDSON STREET, NEW YORK, NY 10014, U.S.A.

PENGUIN GROUP (CANADA), 90 EGLINTON AVENUE EAST, SUITE 700,

TORONTO, ONTARIO M4P 2Y3, CANADA (A DIVISION OF PEARSON PENGUIN CANADA INC.).

PENGUIN BOOKS LTD, 80 STRAND, LONDON WC2R 0RL, ENGLAND.

PENGUIN IRELAND, 25 ST. STEPHEN'S GREEN, DUBLIN 2, IRELAND (A DIVISION OF PENGUIN BOOKS LTD.).

PENGUIN GROUP (AUSTRALIA), 250 CAMBERWELL ROAD, CAMBERWELL, VICTORIA 3124,

AUSTRALIA (A DIVISION OF PEARSON AUSTRALIA GROUP PTY LTD).

PENGUIN BOOKS INDIA PVT LTD, 11 COMMUNITY CENTRE, PANCHSHEEL PARK, NEW DELHI - 110 017, INDIA.

PENGUIN GROUP (NZ), 67 APOLLO DRIVE, ROSEDALE, AUCKLAND 0632,

NEW ZEALAND (A DIVISION OF PEARSON NEW ZEALAND LTD).

PENGUIN BOOKS (SOUTH AFRICA) (PTY) LTD, 24 STURDEE AVENUE, ROSEBANK,

JOHANNESBURG 2196, SOUTH AFRICA.

PENGUIN BOOKS LTD, REGISTERED OFFICES: 80 STRAND, LONDON WC2R 0RL, ENGLAND.

PUBLISHED SIMULTANEOUSLY IN CANADA. PRINTED IN THE UNITED STATES OF AMERICA.

DESIGN BY RYAN THOMANN. TEXT SET IN CC WILD WORDS.

THE ART WAS CREATED IN INK AND COLORED DIGITALLY.

L.C. NUMBER: 2010931550. ISBN 978-0-399-25521-2

1 3 5 7 9 10 8 6 4 2

REX
graphic

TO MIKE CHEN,
FOR MAKING ME A STORYTELLER
INSTEAD OF A DOODLER

IN A WORLD OF SWORDS,
MAGIC, BARBARIANS,
AND EVIL BIG TOES...

5

6

PICK YOUR OWN ARMPITS, YOU SWAMP-WATER GREASE-FISH!

WATCH YOUR MOUTH, BOY! YOUR JOB IN THIS CLAN IS TO SERVE THE WARRIORS!

I *AM* A WARRIOR!

HA! A WARRIOR? YOU'RE JUST A RUNT!

YOU ARE LOWER TO THE GROUND THAN A PUS-FILLED PIMPLE ON THE BELLY OF A SLOP-HOG!

AND MORE USELESS THAN A SWORD MADE OF DONKEY DUNG!

I AM USEFUL! AND I CAN FIGHT! ONE DAY I'LL HAVE MY OWN ARMY!

RIGHT, AN ARMY OF SCRUBBY LITTLE SNOT-NOSED MITES LIKE YOURSELF?

OOOH! I CAN HEAR THE ENEMY SHAKING IN THEIR ARMOR!

9

KEEP THE TOE FROM DROOL...HURRY... IF DROOL GETS HIS TOE, THE CLANS WILL BE DESTROYED... HURRY...DROOL'S ARMY IS CLOSE... VERY CLOSE...

HMMMM...

GRIMEBLADE, YOU WILL GO!

I CANNOT GO! I AM THE BEST SWORDSMAN HERE. YOU NEED ME TO FIGHT!

CLAPPERCLAW, YOU TAKE THE TOE AND GO!

I CANNOT GO! I AM THE BEST AXE SWINGER HERE!

GIZZARDFOOT, YOU GO!

HURRY!

10

12

13

14

15

ZORKO

GORKO

DORKO

DOO!

WOOSH!

THE PASSAGEWAY IS OPEN...ARE YOU READY?

YES, BUT... WHERE AM I GOING?

TO A WORLD THAT IS FAR AWAY AND VERY DIFFERENT FROM OURS. YOU MUST DO AS OTHERS DO. WHEN THE TIME IS RIGHT, WE WILL COME FOR YOU!

WHAT SHOULD I DO WITH THE BIG TOE?

WHACK! CRACK! SMACK! POKE!

CLUNK!

HA! VICTORY IS MINE! HEY...WHAT IS THAT?

ALL THOSE CHILDREN ARE GOING INTO THAT CASTLE. I WILL GO AND BLEND IN...

AND FIND AN ARMY!

OK, KIDS! LINE UP!

HEY! ARE YOU NEW HERE?

YES... I AM...NEW. WHERE AM I?

YOU'RE IN LINE FOR SCHOOL.

SCHOOL?

YEAH. EASTWOOD ELEMENTARY SCHOOL.

IT IS A PALACE!

YEAH, IT'S KINDA BIG. I'LL SHOW YOU WHERE TO GO SO YOU DON'T GET LOST.

THAT IS GOOD OF YOU.

I LIKE YOUR HELMET. IS IT FOR SKATEBOARDING?

NO. FOR WAR!

SWEET! MY NAME'S BILL, WHAT'S YOURS?

I AM FANGBONE.

SWEET! WHOSE CLASS ARE YOU IN?

UH...I AM IN YOUR CLASS, BILL OF EASTWOOD ELEMENTARY SCHOOL.

SWEET. I'LL SHOW YOU WHERE TO GO.

SWEET.

IN CLASS 3G....

MS. GILLIAN, THIS IS FANGBONE. HE'S NEW IN OUR CLASS.

HUH? NO ONE TOLD ME ABOUT A NEW STUDENT.

MAYBE YOU'RE IN THE WRONG CLASS.

HERE, MAKE A NAME TAG FOR NOW.

FANGBONE, CAN YOU WRITE YOUR NAME?

NO.

CAN YOU READ?

NO.

OK...OK...
YOU'RE IN THE RIGHT CLASS.
WELCOME TO 3G. EVERYONE HERE
LEARNS AT THEIR OWN SPEED.

BOYS AND GIRLS?
WE HAVE A NEW
STUDENT IN CLASS.
SAY HI TO FANGBONE.

Hi! Hi! Hi! Yo!

IS FANGBONE YOUR
FIRST OR LAST NAME?

I AM FANGBONE
THE YOUNG, OF THE
MIGHTY LIZARD
CLAN.

SON OF
STEELBEARD
THE BOLD,
GRANDSON TO
LOCKJAW
THE FEARLESS.

GREAT-GRANDSON
OF WEASEL-EYE
THE SLIPPERY!

25

WHY DO YOU HAVE A SWORD?

I AM A WARRIOR! I USE IT TO FIGHT THE ARMY OF DROOL!

WHY DO YOU WEAR THAT HELMET?

TO PROTECT MY SKULL IN BATTLE!

WHY IS YOUR UNDERWEAR MADE OUT OF FUR?

FUR UNDERWEAR IS STUPID.

IT KEEPS ME WARM IN THE FROZEN WINTERS OF SKULLBANIA!

IS SKULLBANIA IN NEW JERSEY?

WHY IS YOUR HAIR SO LONG?

WHAT ARE THOSE THINGS ON YOUR ARMS?

WHY ARE YOUR BOOTS ALL RAGGY?

DO YOU LIKE GLITTER?

CLASS? CLASS! PLEASE RELAX. FANGBONE COMES FROM A FARAWAY PLACE. PEOPLE ARE DIFFERENT ALL OVER THE WORLD. WE MUST RESPECT HIS CULTURE.

BEEP! BEEP! BEEP!

DIBBY, YOU ARE NOT A ROBOT. ASK YOUR QUESTION IN ENGLISH.

WHY DID YOU COME TO OUR SCHOOL?

I AM HERE TO PROTECT THE BIG TOE OF DROOL!

WHAT'S THE BIG TOE OF DROOL?

FIVE HUNDRED WINTERS AGO,
THE GREATEST EVIL THAT EVER LIVED RULED OVER
SKULLBANIA. VENOMOUS DROOL WAS HIS NAME.
HE BUILT AN ARMY THAT SWEPT THROUGH THE LANDS
AND ALMOST WIPED OUT THE CLANS.

MANY BATTLES WERE FOUGHT, AND MANY GREAT
WARRIORS DIED TO KEEP HIS EVIL FROM SPREADING.

FINALLY, DROOL WAS DEFEATED, AND CUT INTO MANY SMALL PIECES...

WHOA! FANGBONE, THIS MIGHT NOT BE APPROPRIATE FOR OUR CLASSROOM.

MORE! MORE!!!

THE PIECES WERE SEPARATED AND TAKEN TO DIFFERENT LANDS
SO THAT VENOMOUS DROOL COULD NEVER RULE AGAIN.

BUT SINCE MY BIRTH, A NEW ARMY OF DROOL WORSHIPERS
HAS BEEN MOVING THROUGH SKULLBANIA, COLLECTING
THE PIECES ONE BY ONE, AND REBUILDING DROOL.

THE ONLY PIECE THAT THEY DO NOT HAVE IS HIS BIG TOE!
MY CLAN WAS PUT IN CHARGE OF PROTECTING THE BIG TOE
BECAUSE IT IS THE MOST EVIL, CURSED, WRETCHED
PART OF HIS BODY.

I WAS GIVEN THE TOE AND SENT INTO YOUR WORLD. VENOMOUS DROOL AND HIS ARMY WILL NEVER FIND ME HERE. HE WILL NEVER GET HIS BIG TOE BACK! **FOR I AM FANGBONE!** **PROTECTOR OF THE BIG TOE OF DROOL!**

32

YES. YOU HAVE TO PLAY. C'MON, IT CAN'T BE THAT BAD.

YOU NEVER GOT BEANED BY DUNCAN MCDUFF.

WINNING IS IMPOSSIBLE.

NOTHING IS IMPOSSIBLE WITH TEAMWORK.

WHAT IF THE WHOLE TEAM STINKS?

CAN WE AT LEAST CHANGE THE NAME OF THE TEAM?

SORRY, WE ALREADY MADE POSTERS AND T-SHIRTS.

BUT EVERYONE LAUGHS AT "EXTREME ATTACK UNICORNS."

EXTREME ATTACK UNICORNS

HEH.

A LITTLE LATER...

BILL, I HAVE TO MAKE.

MAKE WHAT?

MAKE... DROPPINGS.

OH! YOU GOTTA POOP.

MS. GILLIAN, CAN I SHOW FANGBONE THE BOYS' ROOM?

YES.

SEE?

HERE'S THE SINK...

HERE'S THE TOILET...

AND HERE'S THE TP.

YOU MAKE INSIDE? THIS IS MADNESS!

NOT MADNESS. IT'S NORMAL. JUST REMEMBER TO FLUSH.

FLUSH? WHAT IS FLUSH?

AFTER YOU'VE POOPED, YOU HIT THIS LEVER AND ALL THE JUNK GETS SUCKED AWAY.

WOOOOOOOOOOOOSH!

AFTER LUNCH...

37

I DON'T EAT MY BOOGERS!

NO. YOU EAT SWORDBOY'S BOOGERS!

SHUT UP!

HA. ANOTHER FREAK FOR 3G!

THANKS FOR STOPPING ME. I'LL BE SUSPENDED IF I GET INTO ANOTHER FIGHT.

DON'T TALK TO DUNCAN. HE'S THE MEANEST JERK IN THE WHOLE THIRD GRADE.

BILL, WHAT IS A BOOGER-EATER?

DUH. A KID THAT EATS BOOGERS!

BOOGERS? WHAT IS BOOGERS?

Y'KNOW, THE JUNK THAT COMES OUT OF YOUR NOSE.

AH...MY CLAN CALLS THAT "GLOOBUS." THERE WAS ONCE A GREAT WARRIOR LOST IN THE DESERT OF HORRIBLE PAIN FOR TWO WINTERS.

HE SURVIVED BY EATING ONLY HIS GLOOBUS.

AND THE GLOOBUS OF HIS CAMEL.
HE WAS FOREVER AFTER CALLED "GLOOBUS THE GREAT."

BALL! HEADS UP!

WHOOOOOO

AWESOME! WITH YOU ON OUR BEANBALL TEAM, WE COULD ACTUALLY WIN.

WHAT IS THIS BEANBALL YOU SPEAK OF?

IT'S A GAME, LIKE DODGEBALL, BUT THE BALLS ARE SMALLER, AND YOU THROW HARDER.

DO YOU USE SWORDS OR AXES?

NO. JUST BALLS.

WARRIORS DO NOT PLAY GAMES. BESIDES, I DO NOT HAVE TIME. I AM ON A QUEST.

YOU HAVE TO PLAY. YOU'RE IN 3G, AND 3G PLAYS ON FRIDAY.

NO. I NEED ONLY TO PROTECT THE BIG TOE OF DROOL!

...AND BUILD AN ARMY.

AFTER SCHOOL...

BILL, I NEED SOMEWHERE TO SLEEP TONIGHT. DO YOU KNOW OF ANY INNS?

UM... VACATION INN IS OUT ON THE HIGHWAY, BUT YOU NEED A CREDIT CARD.

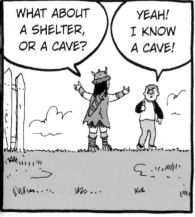

WHAT ABOUT A SHELTER, OR A CAVE?

YEAH! I KNOW A CAVE!

IT'S IN THE WOODS NEAR MY HOUSE. C'MON!

PIK!

POK!

POKE!

GUUHHHHH!!

GET BIG TOE...

BRING TOE TO MIGHTY DROOL...

DESTROY FANGBONE...

AAAAAH!!

BILL! THE BIG TOE IS WIGGLING.

42

43

44

FANGBONE! FOLLOW ME!

PARK

TO THE FOUNTAIN!

SPLASH!

SPLASH!

SPLASH!

45

BY THE AXE OF GLOR, ATTACK US!

FWIP! FWOP! FWOOP!

HA! THE WATER HAS TURNED THEM TO MUD! BILL, YOU ARE A CUNNING WARRIOR!

THANKS. IT WAS JUST TEAMWORK.

AH! TEAMWORK. IT IS THE WAY OF THE WARRIOR. YOU WATCH MY BACK, I WATCH YOURS.

WHERE DID THEY COME FROM?

THEY WERE SENT FROM MY WORLD TO GET THE BIG TOE.

DROOL KNOWS WHERE I AM.

I MUST BUILD MY ARMY QUICKLY!

BILL! YOU WILL BE MY WAR CHIEF. I SHALL CALL YOU **BILL THE BEAST!**

SWEET.

SWEET.

POUND!

A WHILE LATER....

HERE'S THE CAVE.

I WILL BUILD A FIRE.

BUT WE DON'T HAVE ANY--

--MATCHES.

THIS CAVE WILL DO.

BILL THE BEAST, TODAY WAS VERY ODD FOR ME. THIS WORLD IS DIFFERENT FROM MINE. I NEED YOUR HELP.

SURE.

WHERE CAN WE FIND WARRIORS?

GEEZ...I DON'T KNOW. YOU CAN'T JUST BUY AN ARMY AT THE MALL.

THINK ABOUT IT TONIGHT. TOMORROW, WE WILL FIND AN ARMY. THE GREATEST ARMY EVER!

WE WILL CRUSH DROOL AND HIS HORDE INTO DUST THAT WILL BLOW IN THE WIND FOR ALL TIME.

YES, SIR!!

THE NEXT MORNING...

NO, I DON'T WANT TO BE IN YOUR ARMY!

BIKES REPAIR

JUST BECAUSE I'M BIG AND TOUGH-LOOKING AND HAVE TATTOOS, YOU THINK I LIKE FIGHTING? I HATE VIOLENCE! NOW, BEAT IT!

ARENA

HOCKEY PRACTICE 6:00 AM

I'M ALWAYS UP FOR A GOOD FIGHT. WHAT ARE YOU PAYING?

WE HAVE NO GOLD. YOU WILL FIGHT TO STOP EVIL AND DEFEND THE HONOR OF THE CLANS.

SORRY, BOYS, HONOR WON'T BUY ME NEW TEETH.

ARMY RECRUITS

WE WON'T JOIN *YOUR* ARMY, BUT IF YOU WANT TO JOIN OURS, COME BACK WHEN YOU'RE 18.

NOW GET TO SCHOOL!

IF FANGBONE DOESN'T HAVE TO WEAR A SHIRT, NEITHER DO I!

EDDY, IS THAT FUR UNDERWEAR?

IF--

OK. OK. ENOUGH!

WHERE DO YOU EVEN GET FUR UNDERWEAR?

WOW. WHAT'S GOING ON?

YOU'VE GOT FANS, FANGBONE. EVERYONE WANTS TO BE A BARBARIAN!

BARBARIANS ARE STUPID.

GOOD MORNING, MS. GILLIAN.

PRINCIPAL BRUCE!

WHAT'S GOING ON?

THE WHOLE CLASS WANTS TO DRESS LIKE OUR NEW STUDENT FROM SKULLBANIA.

FANTASTIC! LEARNING ABOUT OTHER CULTURES THROUGH THEIR CLOTHING.

BRILLIANT. BRILLIANT! KEEP IT UP, MS. GILLIAN!

IS SKULLBANIA IN NEW JERSEY?

AFTER SCHOOL...

MOM!
I'M HOME!

BILL, YOU LIVE LIKE A KING.

YOUR DWELLING IS MAGNIFICENT.

YOUR DUNGEON MUST BE JUST AS WICKED.

MOM? THIS IS FANGBONE. HE'S A NEW KID IN SCHOOL.

HI.

GREETINGS, MOTHER OF BILL.

HE'S FROM SKULLBANIA.

SKULLBANIA? IS THAT IN NEW JERSEY?

CAN WE HAVE A SNACK?

WHAT'S THE MAGIC WORD?

ZORKO!

GORKO!

DORKO!

DOO!

HUH?

ZORKO!

GORKO!

DORKO!

DOO!

THE MAGIC WORD!

ACTUALLY, THE MAGIC WORD IS "PLEASE."

PAT PAT

WHAT A MYSTERIOUS LAND THIS IS.

BILL, TAKE YOUR MEDICINE!

OK, MOM.

WHAT IS THAT FOR?

SO I DON'T GO ALL HYPER, LIKE BLAAAAAHHH.

IT HELPS ME CONCENTRATE. WANT A SNACK?

SNACK?
WHAT IS SNACK?

I DON'T KNOW. SOMETHING YOU EAT WHEN YOU'RE NOT HUNGRY.

DO YOU HAVE VULTURE BEAK STEW?

NO...
BUT WE HAVE... YES! HOT WINGS!!

THESE ARE MY FAVORITE. TRY THESE.

THEY'RE "ATOMIC" HOT.

THUD!

TOO MUCH, HUH?

THEY ARE WORSE THAN DEMON GLOOBUS.

I THOUGHT A WARRIOR WOULD LIKE THEM.

=CLINK=
=BONK=

HERE. THIS IS MOM'S MEAT LOAF. I THINK IT'S PRETTY GROSS, BUT YOU CAN TRY IT.

AHHHH! THIS IS THE FOOD OF THE GODS!

GREETINGS, MOTHER OF BILL.

FANGBONE SAYS YOUR MEAT LOAF IS BETTER THAN VULTURE BEAK STEW.

I GUESS THAT'S A COMPLIMENT.

WHAT ARE YOU BOYS UP TO?

WE'RE GOING TO FIND AN ARMY.

SOUNDS LIKE FUN. I'LL BE IN THE GARDEN.

MAY YOUR HARVEST BE RICH AND GENEROUS.

I LIKE YOU! YOU'RE FUNNY.

SEE?

NASTY.

EVIL IS NEAR!

BUT THIS TIME, WE'RE READY!

64

68

HA! NOTHING CAN STAND UP TO A WHOLE BUCKET OF ATOMIC WINGS!

BILL THE BEAST! YOU ARE MORE THAN A WAR CHIEF! YOU ARE A SORCERER AS WELL!

COOL. ARE SORCERERS SMART?

THE SMARTEST! YOU MUST BE THE MOST HONORED IN YOUR SCHOOL.

NO WAY. SCHOOL IS FOR KIDS WHO CAN SIT AT A DESK ALL DAY WITHOUT MOVING.

SIT! SIT! SIT! AND YOU HAVE TO KNOW ONLY THE ANSWERS THE TEACHER WANTS. THEY DON'T CARE IF YOU KNOW OTHER THINGS. LIKE HOW TO STOP A HOUND-SNAKE.

MAGGOT TEETH!

71

DUUUDE! YOUR AIM IS PERFECT. YOU GOTTA PLAY BEANBALL!

WE COULD SO TOTALLY WIN!

I TOLD YOU, BILL, WARRIORS DO NOT PLAY GAMES.

YOU MAY BE A WARRIOR, BUT YOU'RE A KID, TOO. KIDS PLAY GAMES.

I AM NOT PLAYING.

IN THE CLASSROOM...

OK, BOYS AND GIRLS... THE OTHER DAY WE WERE TALKING ABOUT THE EARTH. DOES ANYONE REMEMBER WHY IT LOOKS LIKE THE SUN "RISES" IN THE MORNING?

FANGBONE?

MANY THOUSANDS OF WINTERS AGO, THE WORLD WAS TOTALLY DARK. A BEAUTIFUL BUT EVIL PRINCESS NAMED ZIZZELLA RULED OVER THE ENTIRE LAND.

A GREAT WARRIOR NAMED STONEBACK THE SOLID ASKED ZIZZELLA TO MARRY HIM. SHE AGREED, BUT ONLY IF HE COULD BRING HER THE EYE OF THE CYCLOPTOPUS.

FOR YEARS, STONEBACK SEARCHED FOR THE FEARSOME CYCLOPTOPUS, WHICH WAS HARD TO FIND IN A WORLD THAT WAS TOTALLY DARK. FINALLY HE FOUND IT, SLAYED IT, AND RETURNED WITH THE EYE.

BUT ZIZZELLA NEVER WANTED TO MARRY STONEBACK.
SHE THOUGHT THAT THE CYCLOPTOPUS WOULD EAT HIM
AND HE WOULD NEVER RETURN. WHEN HE SHOWED UP FOR
THE WEDDING, SHE AND HER SUBJECTS WERE GONE.

STONEBACK WAS FURIOUS! HE VOWED TO FIND HER.
BUT IT WAS EASY TO HIDE IN A WORLD THAT WAS ALWAYS
DARK. IN A RAGE, STONEBACK SET THE
CYCLOPTOPUS EYE ON FIRE AND
KICKED IT INTO THE SKY.

THE EYE
LIT UP THE LAND,
AND DAY WAS CREATED.

EVERY DAY, STONEBACK THE SOLID KICKS THE BURNING EYE INTO THE SKY AND SEARCHES FOR ZIZZELLA!

THAT'S QUITE A STORY, FANGBONE.

IT IS NOT A STORY. IT IS TRUTH.

BUT IT'S NOT THE ANSWER WE WERE LOOKING FOR, FANGBONE. ACTUALLY, THE EARTH ROTATES.

ROTATES? NONSENSE.

MS. GILLIAN? YOU SAID THAT WE HAVE TO ACCEPT OTHER PEOPLE'S CULTURES AND THE THINGS THAT THEY THINK. RIGHT?

YES, BUT...

WELL, IF THAT'S WHAT FANGBONE THINKS, THAT'S WHAT I THINK!

GIANT BURNING EYES ARE MUCH COOLER THAN ROTATION.

ROTATION IS LAME.

STONEBACK IS STUPID.

HOW DO YOU SPELL "CYCLOPTOPUS?"

79

BEEP! BEEP! BEEP! I AM STONEBACK!

I BET ZIZZELLA LIKED GLITTER!

OK. OK! THE SUN IS A GIANT BURNING EYE!

AND IT'S KICKED INTO THE SKY BY AN ANGRY BARBARIAN. WRITE THAT IN YOUR NOTEBOOKS!

WOW. LOOK AT ALL THESE HARD WORKERS. GREAT JOB, MISS GILLIAN.

LIKE THE BOOTS?

=PIK=
=PIK=
=PIK=

EDDY, GET THAT PENCIL OUT OF YOUR NOSE.

BUT IT'S MY CULTURE.

NO, IT'S NOT. IT'S JUST GROSS.

IN THE SCHOOL YARD...

HEY, SWORDBOY, WHERE DO YOU COME FROM?

I COME FROM SKULLBANIA!

SKULL-LAME-IA? NEVER HEARD OF IT. IT MUST BE LAME.

YOU MAKE NO SENSE.

YOU ARE NOTHING BUT PESKY VERMIN.

SHUT UP OR I'LL HIT YOU!

HA! *YOU* HIT *ME?* I'VE BEEN IN THE JAWS OF A VIPER-CAT, FELT THE SPIT OF A FLAME-BULL. I DO NOT FEAR YOU.

SHUT UP, OR I'LL DO IT!

YOU ARE WEAK. YOUR PUNCH WOULD BE THAT OF A TIRED BABY.

BABY? I'M A THIRD-GRADER!

I AM A THIRD GRADER TOO...WITH A SWORD.

AFTER DROOL WAS CUT UP AND THE PIECES SEPARATED, HIS HEAD WAS PLACED IN A GUARDED TEMPLE.

THE GUARDS BEGAN TO PLAY GAMES. DROOL'S FOLLOWERS SNUCK IN AND WERE ABLE TO STEAL THE HEAD...

...WITHOUT EVEN A BATTLE.

IT IS THE MOST SHAMEFUL MOMENT IN ALL OF HISTORY.

WELL, THAT'S NOT GOING TO HAPPEN HERE.

I CANNOT HELP YOU, BILL THE BEAST.

IT'S JUST BILL! BILL THE **LOSER!** HAVEN'T YOU NOTICED? DON'T YOU GET IT? 3G IS THE **LOSER CLASS!** THEY CALL US DORKS AND BOOGER-EATERS AND EVERYONE LAUGHS AT US AND WE NEVER WIN AT ANYTHING, *'CAUSE WE'RE JUST A BUNCH OF MESSED-UP LOSERS!!!*

FORGET IT! ALL YOU CARE ABOUT IS THAT STUPID BIG TOE OF DROOL!

WELL, IF THAT'S WHAT FANGBONE THINKS, THAT'S WHAT I THINK.

BILL! YOU ARE NOT A LOSER. YOU ARE A WARRIOR, AND A FRIEND.

BUT YOU SAID YOU CAN'T PLAY.

YOU HAVE WATCHED MY BACK, NOW I WILL WATCH YOURS. I WILL FIGHT WITH YOU! WE WILL DESTROY OUR ENEMIES. THE CHILDREN OF THEIR CHILDREN WILL FEAR US!

WHOA. WE JUST WANT TO WIN.

IF WE LOSE, ARE WE LEFT IN THE PIT OF SHAME WITH A TWO-TAILED SCORPION?

NO. WE GET A JUICE BOX.

TWEET!

ALL RIGHT! ARE THE TEAMS READY? YOU KNOW THE RULES! IF YOU GET HIT, YOU'RE OUT, AND THE FIRST TEAM WITH NO PLAYERS LEFT LOSES. IF YOU CATCH THE BALL, THE THROWER IS OUT. AND NO THROWING AT THE FACE!

WINNER!
EXTREME ATTACK UNICORNS!

ROUND TWO. EXTREME ATTACK UNICORNS VS. DINO-BALLERS.

TWEET!

BOOM!

POOM!

DONK!

POP!

BAM!

92

OK, GUYS! TEAMWORK...3...2...1...

94

BIP! BAM! BAM! POW!

WINNER, AND CHAMPIONS! EXTREME ATTACK UNICORNS!

BILL! THE TOE IS WIGGLING MORE THAN EVER! A GREAT EVIL IS CLOSE!

WE HAVE BEATEN MONSTERS TWICE. THIS NEXT MONSTER WILL BE THE STRONGEST YET.

98

105

106

EVIL IS STUPID!

117

MONDAY MORNING...

GOOD MORNING, CHAMPIONS! I HAVE SOMETHING FOR ALL OF YOU.

I'M A WINNER!

I'M A WINNER!

I'M A WINNER!

AND FOR YOU, FANGBONE, I HAVE A SPECIAL ONE, "MOST VALUABLE PLAYER."

MOST VALUABLE PLAYER!

THANK YOU, BUT IT IS BILL THE BEAST, THE WAR CHIEF AND SORCERER, WHO IS MOST VALUABLE.

MOST VALUABLE PLAYER!

I'M A WINNER!

MOST VALUABLE PLAYER!

I'M A WINNER!

AND TO MY ARMY...

MY CLAN AND I OWE YOU A LIFE DEBT.

WITH YOU AT MY SIDE, WE CAN PROTECT THE BIG TOE OF DROOL FROM ANY VILE, HORRIBLE, WICKED, FOUL BEAST THAT VENOMOUS DROOL CAN THROW AT US! BE IT A TIGER-DRAGON, GORILLA-TROLL, OR LAVA-FERRET! WE SHALL FIGHT TO DEFEND THE HONORABLE CLANS OF SKULLBANIA! NO MATTER IF WE ARE EATEN, CRUSHED, TORTURED, OR PULLED LIMB FROM LIMB, WE WILL FIGHT!

FIGHT! FIGHT!

OK...BUT WE HAVE A QUIZ FIRST.

QUIZ? WHAT IS QUIZ?

THE END

MICHAEL REX IS THE AUTHOR AND ILLUSTRATOR OF OVER TWENTY BOOKS FOR CHILDREN, INCLUDING THE **NEW YORK TIMES** #1 BESTSELLER **GOODNIGHT GOON**. MICHAEL HAS A MASTER'S DEGREE IN VISUAL ARTS EDUCATION (K-12), AND WORKED AS A NEW YORK CITY ART TEACHER FOR FOUR YEARS. HE VISITS SCHOOLS ACROSS THE COUNTRY, AND HAS APPEARED ON **THE CELEBRITY APPRENTICE** AS A GUEST ILLUSTRATOR.

MIKE LIVES IN THE BRONX WITH HIS WIFE AND THEIR TWO BOYS.

BRACE YOURSELF FOR BOOK TWO OF
FANGBONE!
THIRD-GRADE BARBARIAN . . .

THE EGG OF MISERY